ICKY WORLD

WE NEED POOP!

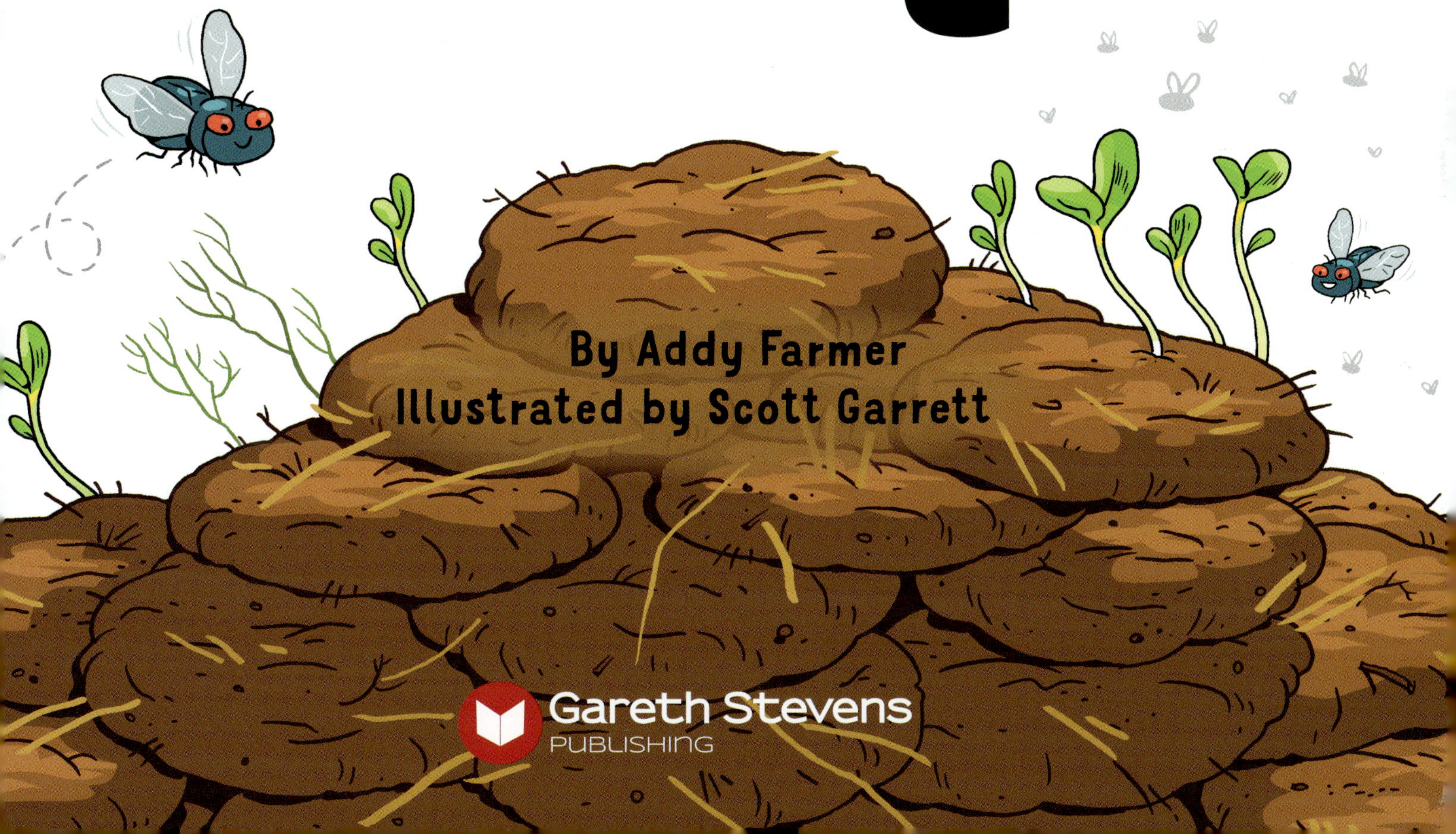

By Addy Farmer
Illustrated by Scott Garrett

Gareth Stevens
PUBLISHING

Please visit our website, www.garethstevens.com. For a free color catalog of all our high-quality books, call toll free 1-800-542-2595 or fax 1-877-542-2596.

Cataloging-in-Publication Data
Names: Farmer, Addy. | Garrett, Scott.
Title: We need poopp! / Addy Farmer, illustrated by Scott Garrett.
Description: Buffalo, NY : Gareth Stevens Publishing, 2026. | Series: Icky world | Includes glossary and index.
Identifiers: ISBN 9781482473001 (pbk.) | ISBN 9781482473018 (library bound) | ISBN 9781482473025 (ebook)
Subjects: LCSH: Feces--Juvenile literature. | Animal droppings--Juvenile literature. | Feces--Miscellanea--Juvenile literature.
Classification: LCC QP159.F376 2026 | DDC 612.3'6--dc23

Published in 2026 by
Gareth Stevens Publishing
2544 Clinton St.
Buffalo, NY 14224

First published in Great Britain in 2023 by Wayland

Series Editor: Grace Glendinning
Series Designer: Peter Scoulding

Printed in the United States of America

CPSIA compliance information: Batch #CSGS26: For further information contact Gareth Stevens at 1-800-542-2595.

CONTENTS

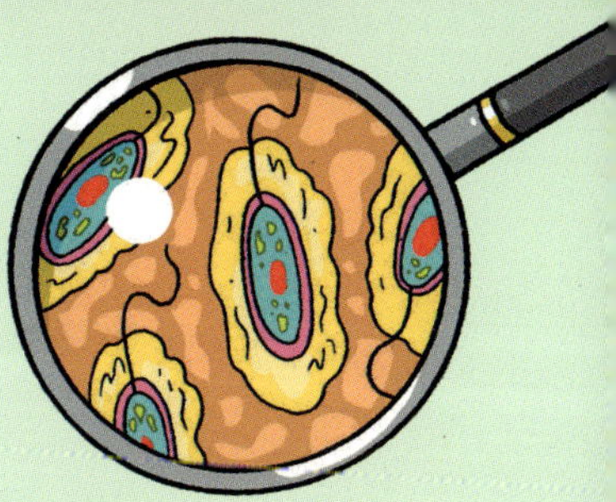

What on Earth is Poop?

**Feces, excrement, dung, stools, scat—
there are so many different words for poop!**

But what *IS* it? And why do scatologists (scientists who study poop) think it's so fascinating?

Poop-EE!

Poop is the waste bits of food an animal can't digest, such as seeds and fiber, all mixed up with water, bacteria, and slimy mucus.

All animals poop, from the tiniest speck of fly poop to the blue whale's huge plume of poop.

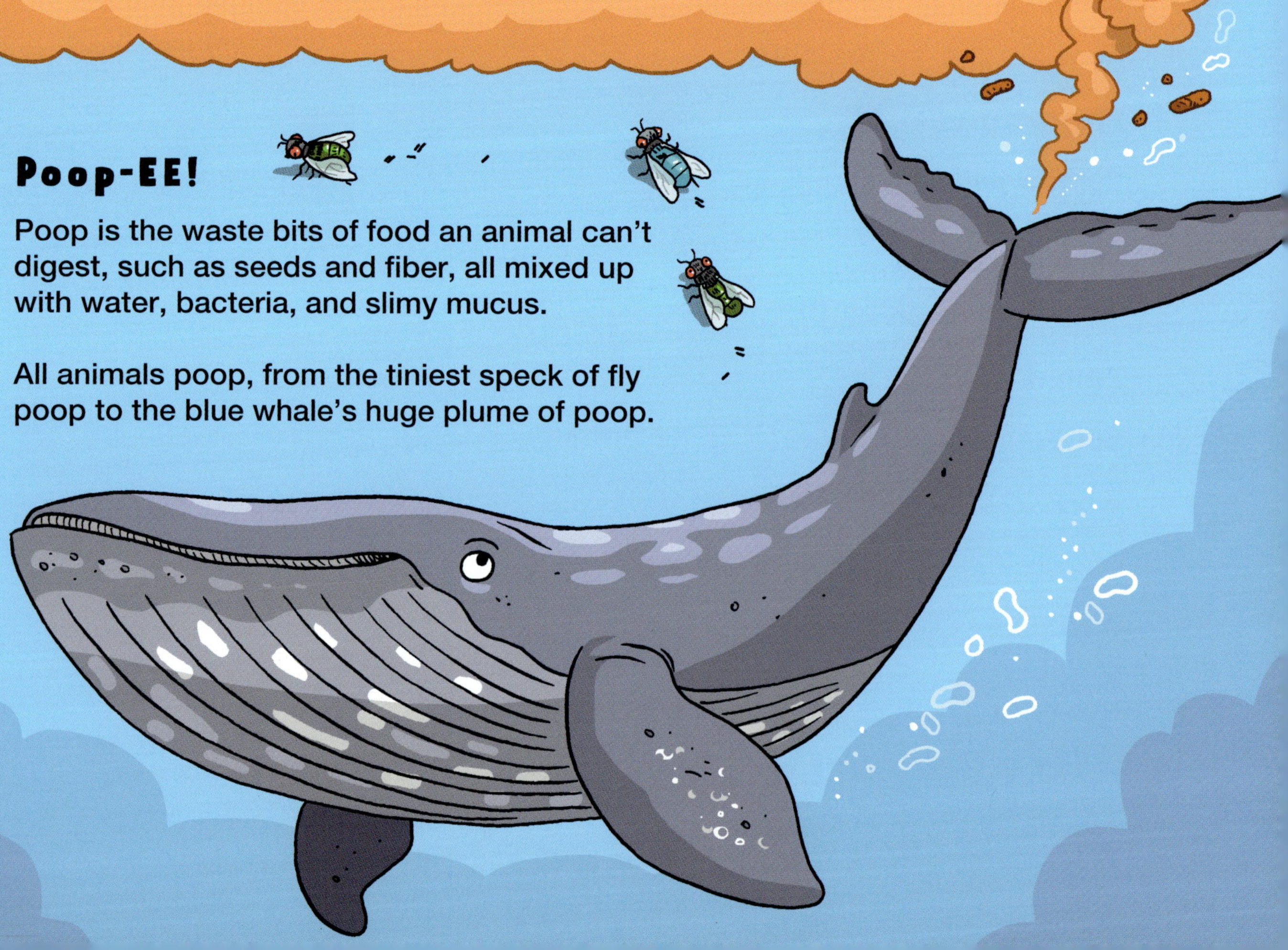

People poop

Let's not forget about human poop! Humans across Earth poop about 640 billion pounds (290 billion kg) per year. Add in all the other animal poop, and it can lead to a whole heap of poop problems, from disease to pollution.

All this poop has to go somewhere!

So, what we do with our poop matters.

Eat, poop, renew!

In this book, we'll learn from amazing animals who eat, poop, and renew in habitats across the world.

We'll also see how poop can do vital work in keeping the world's ecosystems in balance.

Yes, poop can be smelly and gross–nature's way of keeping us away from potential disease–but it can also be useful, from farming to building.

Poop is information!

Scientists who study prehistoric poop, which are called coprolites, have made lots of important discoveries about how animals lived millions of years ago.

Big dinosaurs did big poop! The **Argentinosaurus** ate lots of plants and pooped out more than 44 pounds (20 kg) at a time.

What dino ate for dinner

Poke about in a coprolite and you may find bits of bone, teeth, and claws. This dino was definitely a meat eater!

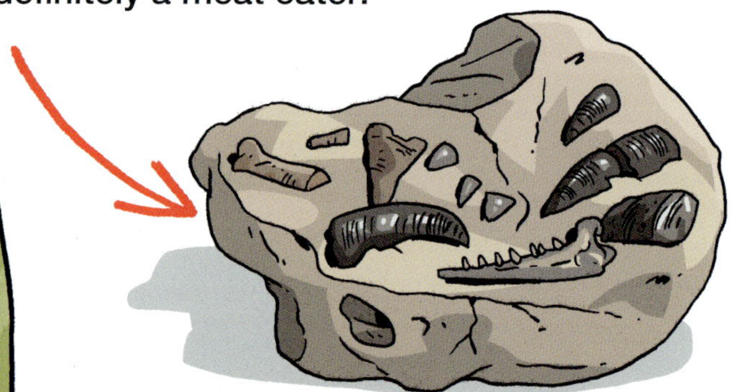

About 75 million years ago the **Hadrosaurus** that pooped this out grazed on leaves, wood, and fungi.

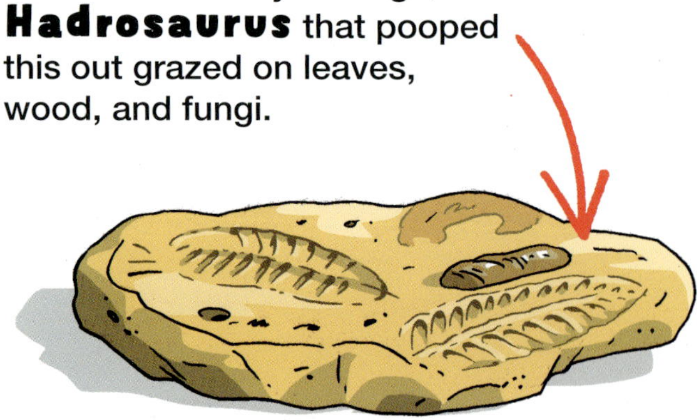

Dino poop ecosystem

All that dinosaur poop was a source of food for smaller animals and insects, and for bacteria. And the poop played an important part in making Earth's early soil a healthy mix for early plant life.

Dino poop and its poop-eating friends helped keep prehistoric vegetation lush and green by adding nutrients back into the soil.

Creature shout-out: DUNG BEETLE

There are thousands of different types of dung beetle found on every continent (except Antarctica), and each is a poop pro! They are skilled **decomposers**.

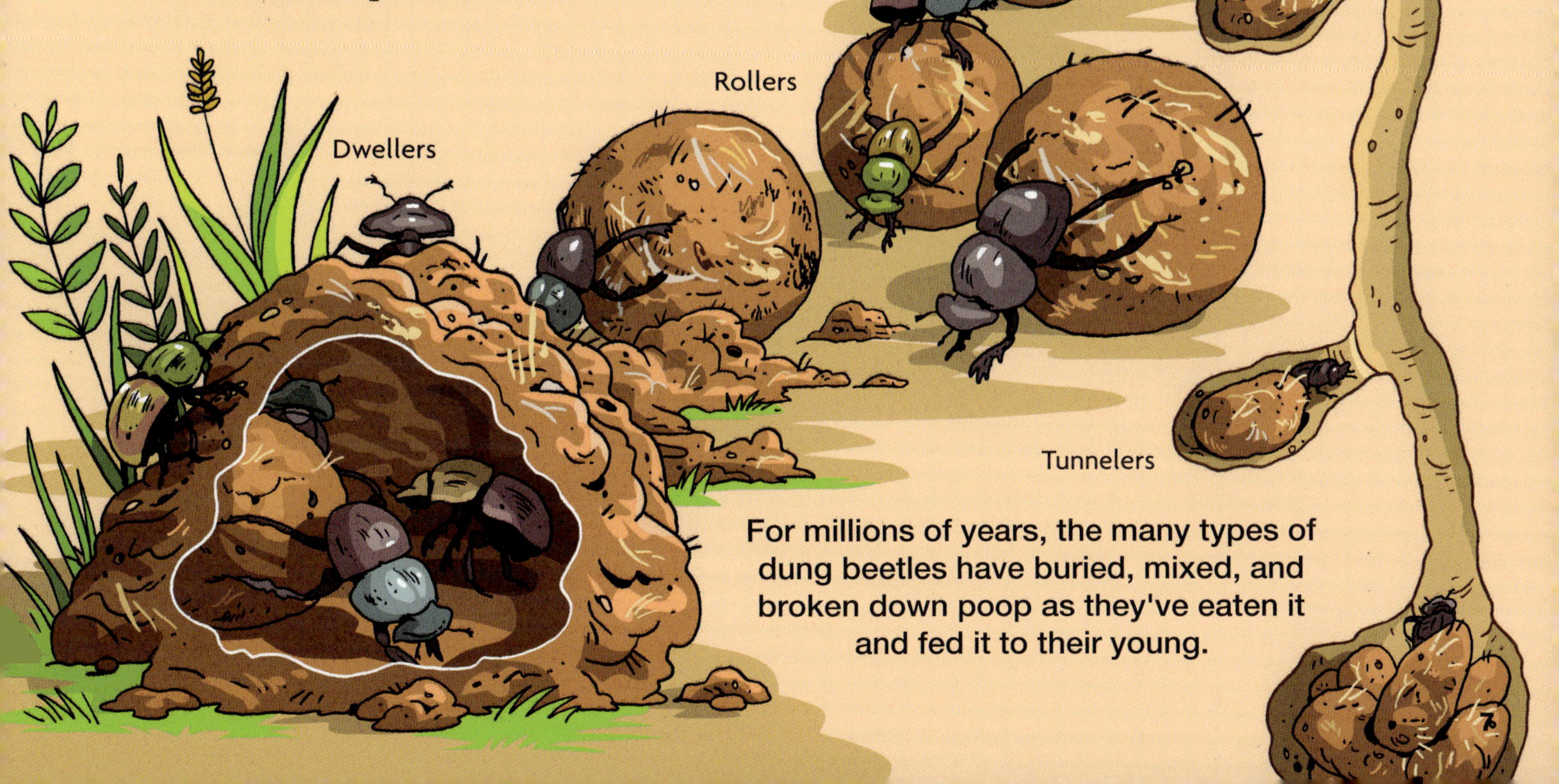

For millions of years, the many types of dung beetles have buried, mixed, and broken down poop as they've eaten it and fed it to their young.

Plants love poop

**How do the world's plants grow?
With the help of poop!**

Fantastic fertilizer

Animal poop all over the world today acts as a fertilizer for Earth's soil. This helps plants grow faster and stronger. How does this work?

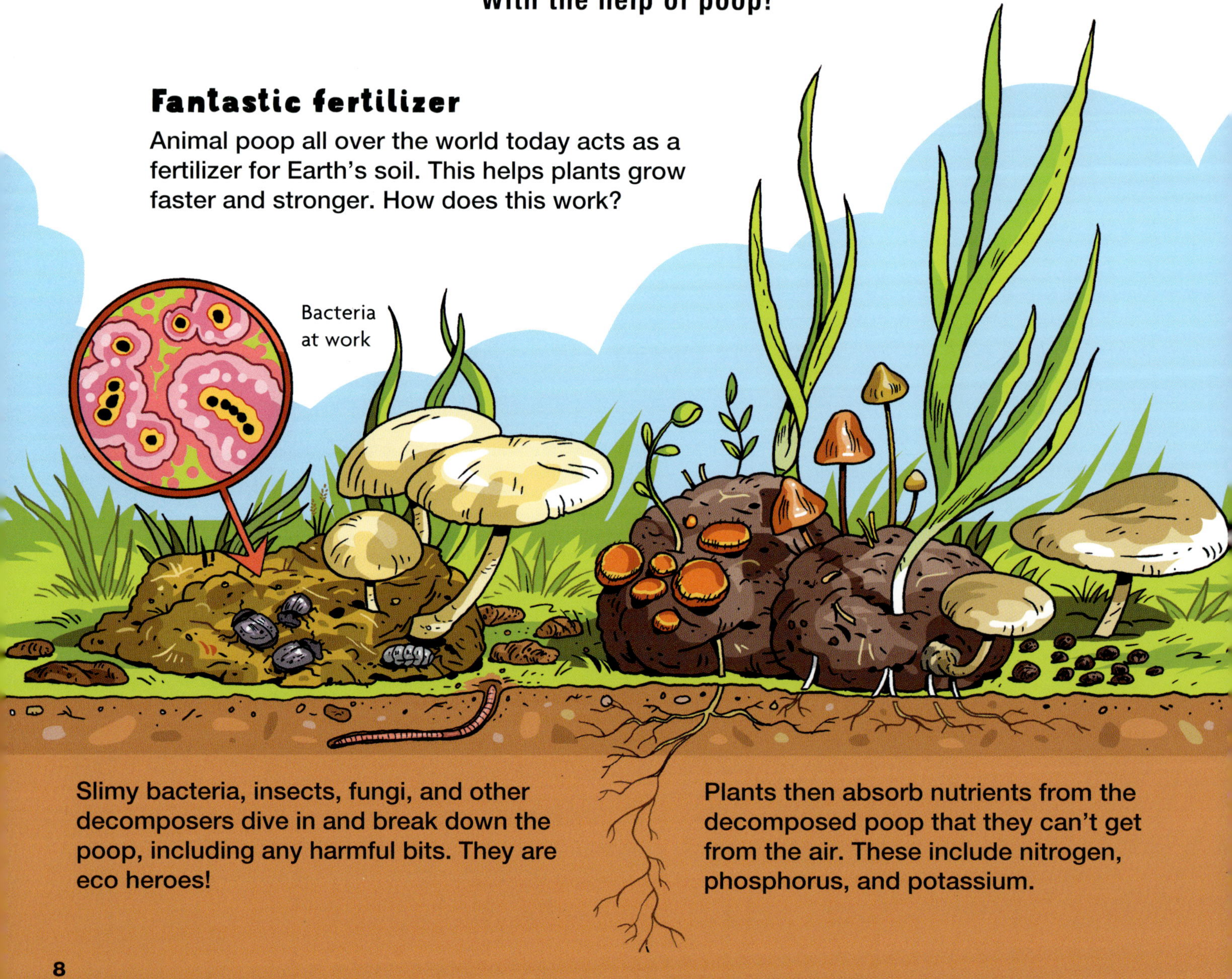

Slimy bacteria, insects, fungi, and other decomposers dive in and break down the poop, including any harmful bits. They are eco heroes!

Plants then absorb nutrients from the decomposed poop that they can't get from the air. These include nitrogen, phosphorus, and potassium.

Poop on the farm

Farmers also use livestock poop to grow crops for us to eat.

Animal poop can be spread over fields as solid manure, as compost (poop mixed with other natural waste) or as slurry (liquified animal poop sprayed by machine).

Solid manure

Compost mix

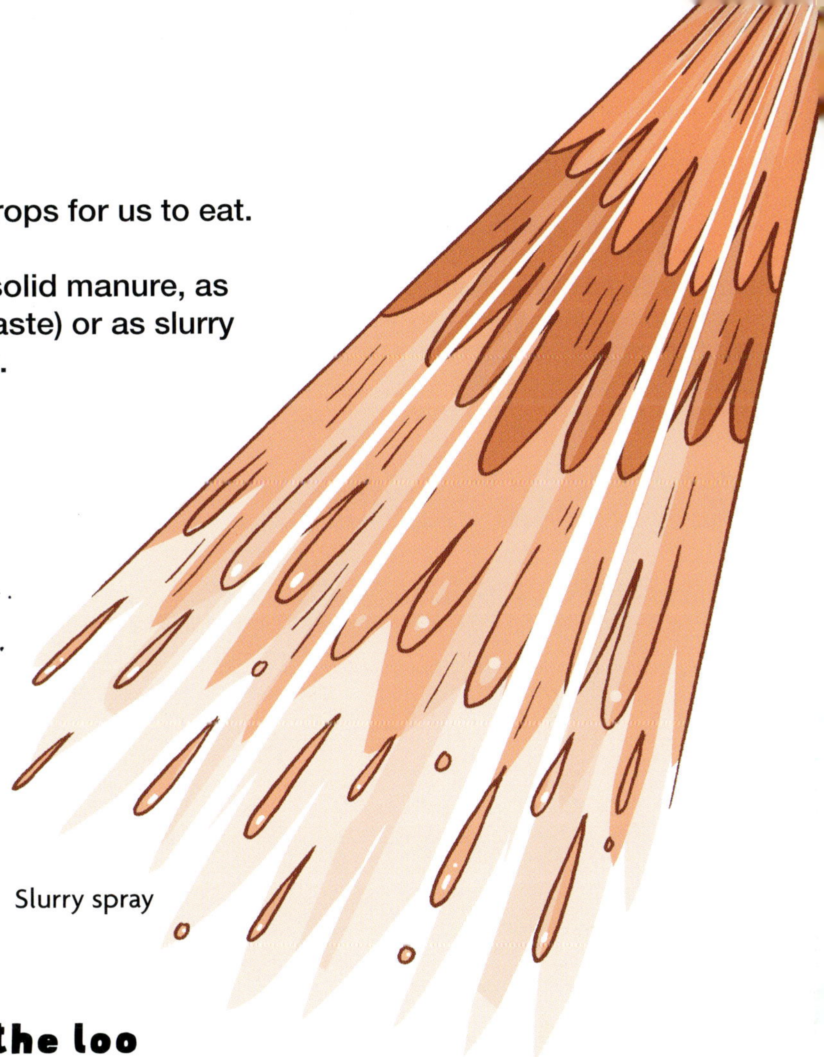
Slurry spray

Poop in the loo

Some farmers have found a way to make good use of all the human-made poop too.

To make it safe for using on food crops, human poop has to be composted. It gets mixed up with plant waste, and then helpful microbes work away, which kills harmful bacteria.

What's left is a safe and rich fertilizer!

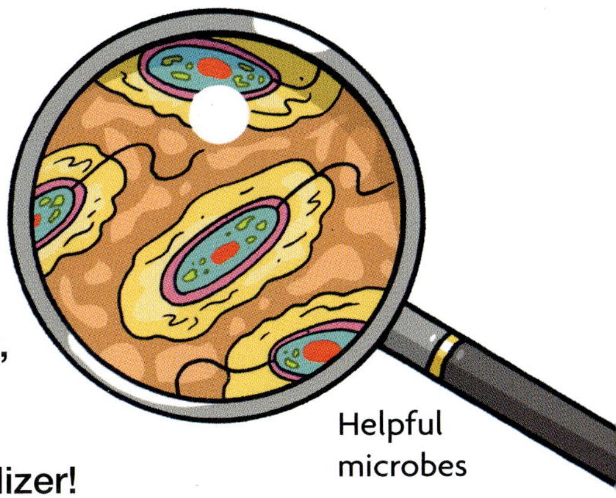
Helpful microbes

Ocean poop

Sea poopers help to maintain the health of the world's oceans.

Sea cucumbers suck up sand, filter out the waste, then poop out cleaner sand. This means that fish can breathe more easily and that seagrasses, corals, and shellfish can thrive on a healthy ocean floor.

Parrotfish eat slimy algae off coral reefs and poop it out as sand. (Walk on the famous white sand beaches of Hawaii and you're walking on parrotfish poop!)

Here's the biggy!

Whale poop is like a global fertilizer. Mineral-rich whale poop feeds the ocean's plants and animals, and even humans. It's an eco poop loop!

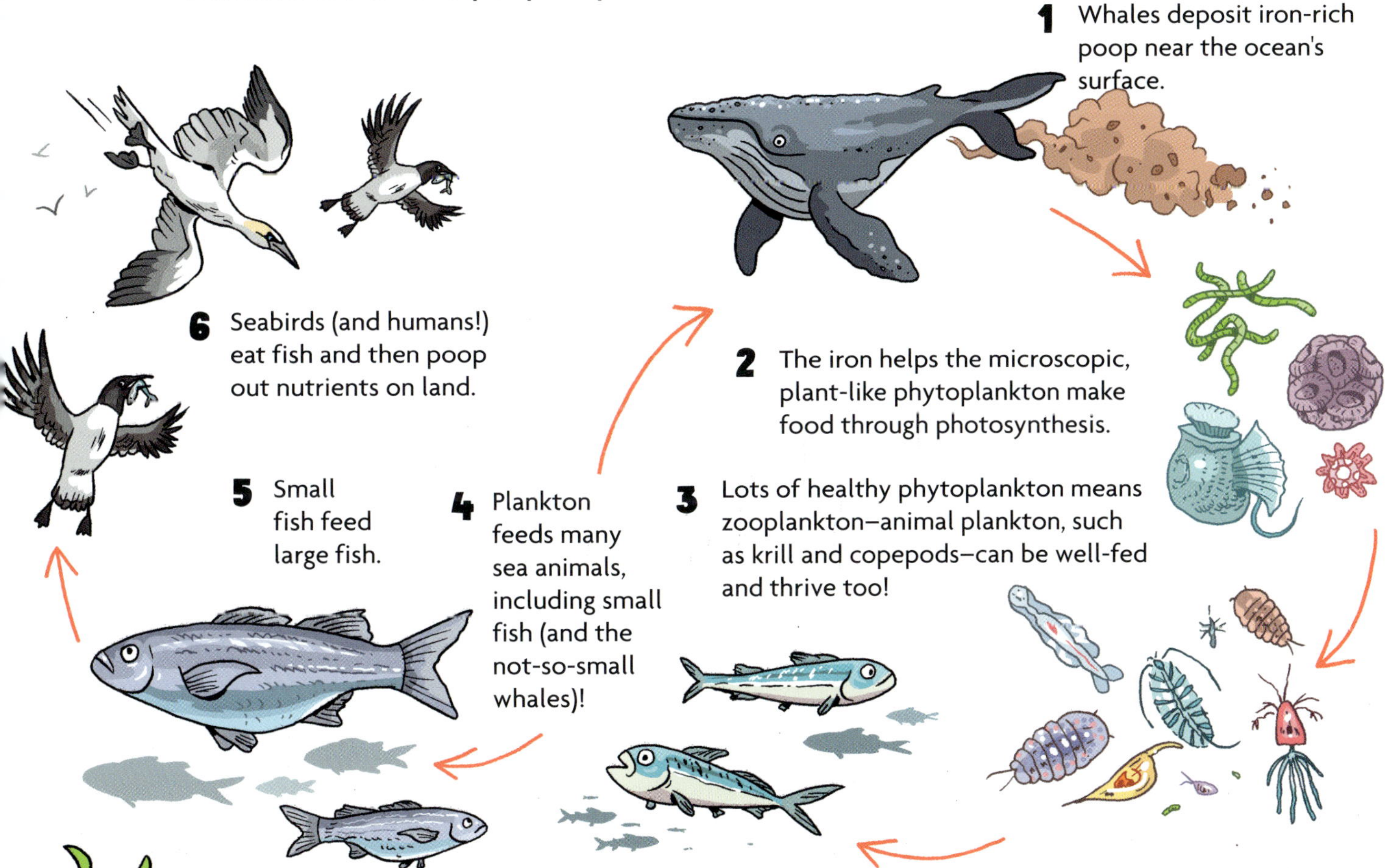

The poop that just keeps giving

Healthy ocean plants suck in more than half of the world's carbon dioxide (CO_2), which helps our climate stay cool. They couldn't do it without whale poop!

Poop delivery!

Animal poop is used as a travel service for plants to send their seeds far and wide. It's also a nutritious delivery for some clever carnivorous plants.

Poop builds biodiversity: in the sea, on land, and up in the trees!

The **tambaqui**, also known as the vegetarian piranha, eats fruit that has fallen into the water from the trees of the Amazon rainforest. It eventually poops out the seeds, where currents can carry it up to 3 miles (5 km) away.

Birds such as **robins** and **thrushes** love to eat mistletoe berries. As they pass through the birds, the mistletoe seeds get super sticky. This means they can cling to the next tree they land on as poop.

The new mistletoe plant will sprout from cracks in the bark where they land.

Bears eat lots of fruit. The seeds grow into plants in new places, and the plant growth is helped along by the poop fertilizer at the same time.

Make a deposit, please

Pitcher plants in South America have specially shaped leaves that bounce back **bat** squeaks, attracting bats to come, sit, eat, and poop! The poop is a source of food for the plant.

Another type of pitcher plant makes sugary secretions to lure in **tree shrews** and **rats**, who then leave some poopy goodness behind.

Poop as the animals do

What do animals do with all their poop?

Many baby animals, such as **elephants** or **hippo** calves, eat their mums' poop! It introduces healthy gut microbes for digesting tough-to-eat leaves.

The poop web: it's not just for baby elephants

A poop feast feeds into many ecosystems!

Elephants eat lots of leaves and do a lot of big poop!

Along come the dung beetles and other decomposer insects.

The insects attract amphibians, such as frogs ...

... or other animals, such as meerkats and honey badgers, who also scavenge elephant feces for tasty insect morsels.

Whatever is left over goes into the soil to help plants grow lots of delicious leaves ... for the elephants to eat!

Herbivores, such as **zebras** and **cows**, leave one-third of the nutrients they get from their food in their poop. They eat it again to get all the bits missed the first time.

The **southern cassowary** eats cassowary plums, which are barely digested the first time. They come out as yummy chunks of fruit. Dig in again!

Guinea pigs and **rabbits** occasionally make especially nutritious poop called cecotropes. They often eat them straight from their own bottoms. Yum bum!

Prey or predator?

Animals use poop to fight, hide, or disguise.

Brazilian skipper butterfly larvae can shoot their feces, called frass, up to 6.5 feet (2 m) away. Stay away!

Hoopoe chicks can squirt a jet of poop, which they aim right at the eyes of potential predators.

Hoopoe chick shooting poop from its nest

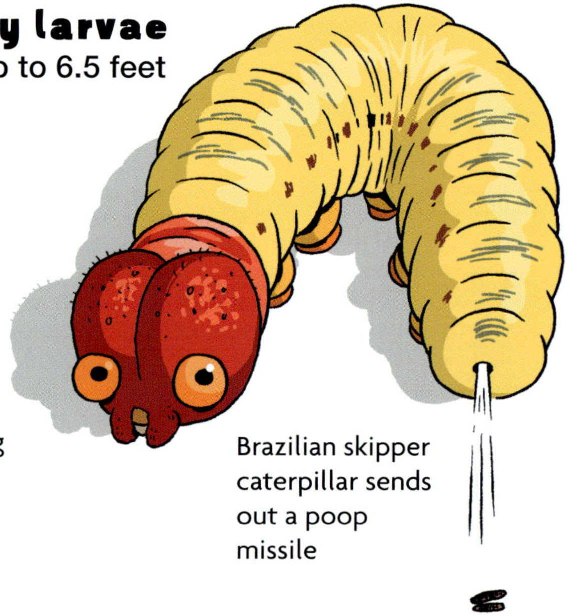

Brazilian skipper caterpillar sends out a poop missile

Ballistic poop

Throughout history, even humans have used poop as a weapon to fling at enemies–much like our **ape** relatives still do today!

Sneaky poop disguise

Lions, wolves, and **jackals** roll in strong-smelling poop to mask their scents, so they can sneak up on their prey.

Poop can be a lifesaver!

The **pygmy sperm whale** hides from its enemies in its own cloud of poop.

Dung spiders and some **caterpillars** have evolved to *look like* poop to ward off predators.

The **potato beetle** covers itself in toxic poop to avoid being eaten.

Poop news

Poop can be an important method of communication for wildlife.

Marking territory

"Clear off! This is my place!" Sometimes poop sends a very strong message about where an animal has claimed its home.

Wombats spread their square-shaped poop around their territory each day to warn others away.

Some species of **rhino** do similar, but they go one step further: They shuffle their back feet in the poop so everywhere they walk leaves a scent trail.

Find your way by poop

The **hippo** leaves a trail of dung to find its way back home.

Poop chats

Pooping leaves a strong and unique scent, which can be a positive thing too.

Two-toed sloths create poop heaps, called dung middens, to establish mating sites for themselves and for the moths that live in their coats. How generous!

Some creatures, such as **genets** and **lemurs**, create "bathrooms" in a raised area and leave messages for relatives and potential mates in this central, protected location.

Giant otters build community toilets too–on river banks.

Otter groups hang out in this bathroom a lot, learning important information about each other from their poop, and marking their group's territory for passing rivals.

Poop homes

Some animals will live in whatever poop they think will make a good home.

The **secretary bird** uses zebra poop to stick together its nest.

Oven birds make mud nests, but will also use antelope poop when mud is in short supply.

Millipedes make a nest for their eggs from tiny poop bricks left behind by insects.

Special mention: cuckoo spit! While it's not strictly poop, it does come out of the **froghopper nymph's** bottom. These nymphs blow air through a liquid to create foam (all with their bums), so that they can hide inside it from predators.

Termites are known for building whole mounds of poop to live in. But they also *garden* with poop and grow fantastic fungi for their young to eat.

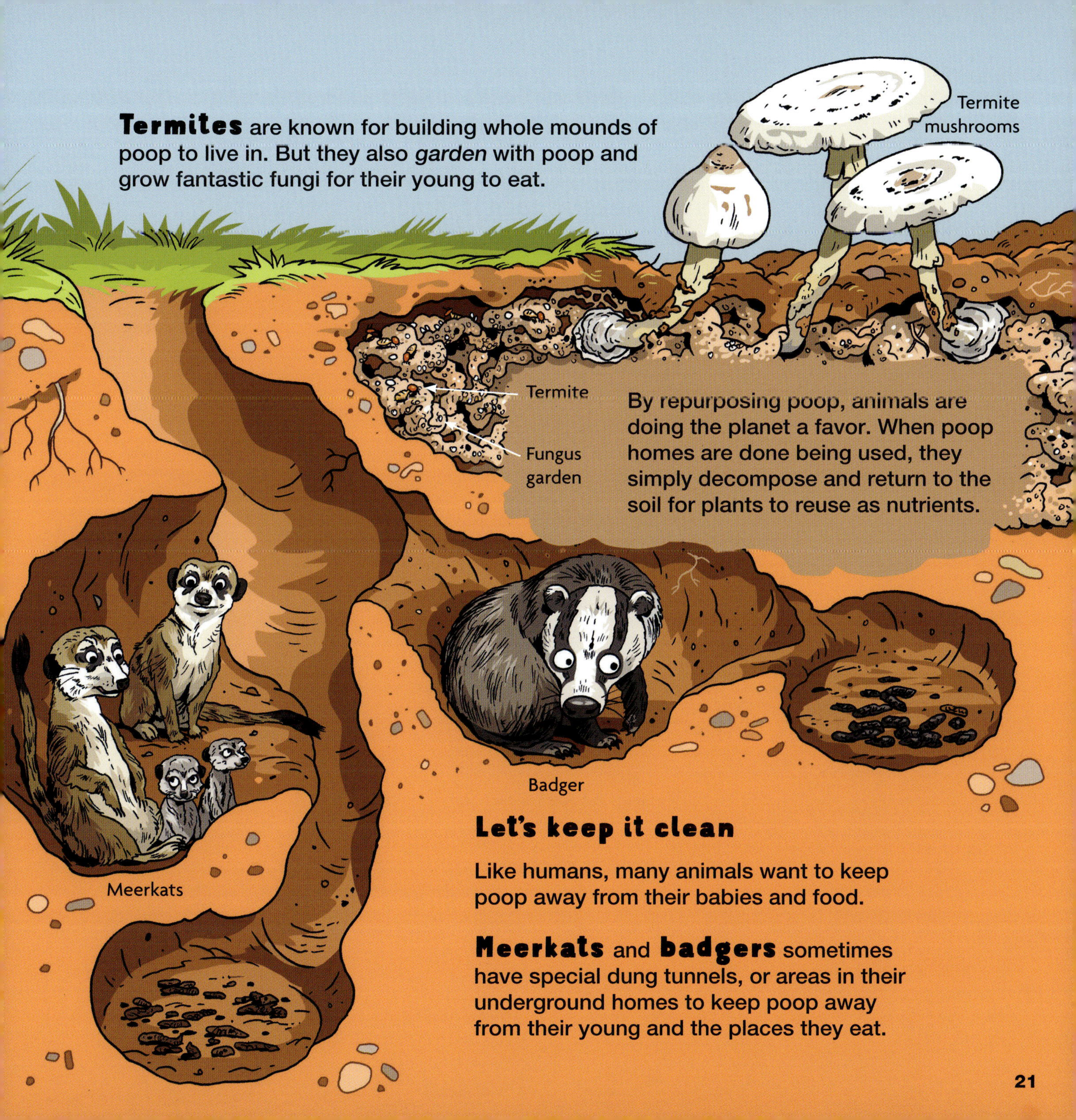

By repurposing poop, animals are doing the planet a favor. When poop homes are done being used, they simply decompose and return to the soil for plants to reuse as nutrients.

Let's keep it clean

Like humans, many animals want to keep poop away from their babies and food.

Meerkats and **badgers** sometimes have special dung tunnels, or areas in their underground homes to keep poop away from their young and the places they eat.

Humans use poop too

Humans tend to think of poop as smelly and disgusting but, like other animals, we have used it in all sorts of ways!

We want your poop

Throughout history, bird poop called guano has been collected as a valuable fertilizer and for use in weaponry. There was even a war fought over it.

1860s: Chile, Peru, and Spain fought a war over possession of the guano-covered Chincha Islands.

Poop plaster

In many parts of the world, dung is mixed with clay to make wall plaster, or mixed with mud to make flooring. It is very strong and long-lasting!

Poop food

Many delicacies can be enjoyed thanks to poop. Lots of people drink coffee made from coffee beans pooped out by a civet, or tea leaves pooped out by a caterpillar.

And a limited-edition batch of elephant-poop-coffee-flavored beer sold out quickly to many eager customers.

Powered by poop

Scientists have developed machines called biodigesters, which break down poop and create a fuel called biogas. This can be used to light and heat up homes, cars, and buses.

Energy made from the animal poop at Canada's Toronto Zoo feeds right into the city's electricity supply. In the UK, one inventor figured out a way to use dog poop energy to keep street lights running!

Poop renews all day long

Poop possibilities are endless! It's been converted into biodegradable plastics, water filters, and even paper. And because poop is inescapable, it's a highly renewable resource.

Bioplastic bottle

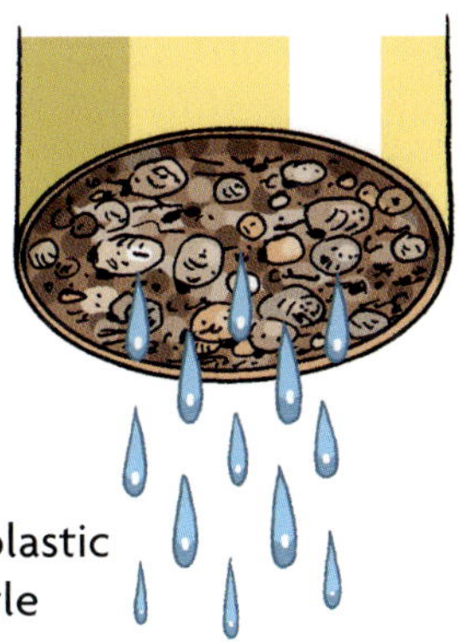

Llama poop water filter

Elephant poop paper

Poop problems

Too much poop can pollute the environment and also cause disease. Humans must deal with our poop wisely to avoid disaster.

Our poop, our problem

Untreated poop attracts flies and spreads diseases, such as typhoid and cholera. To prevent disease, many parts of the world have toilets and sewers to take the waste away from living areas.

But, human poop still causes disease around the world. About 1.8 billion people do not have access to a sanitary toilet or sufficient waste treatment systems, which can mean that poop gets into the drinking water.

And it's not just bacteria and disease–some medicines, bits of which are pooped out, end up in the food chain if we don't deal with poop carefully. This can lead to new diseases that can resist medicines, or to animals getting sick from having human medicine in their digestive systems.

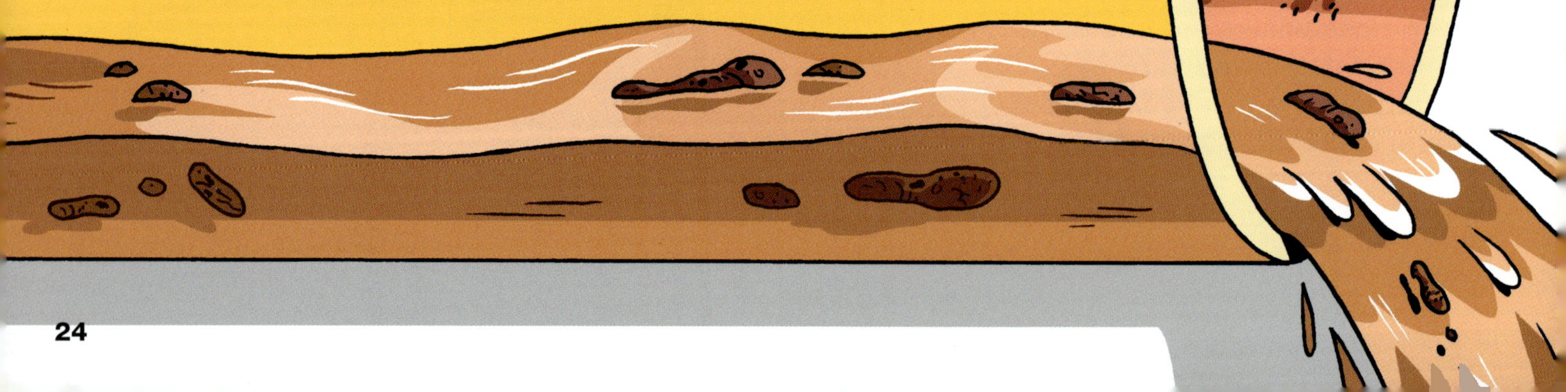

Dung can bung up the atmosphere and rivers

The world's livestock produces billions of tons of poop every year. Methane gas from all the decaying poop is a significant cause of climate change.

Excess poop from so many farm animals can also lead to the pollution of soil and water if not dealt with properly or reduced.

Rivers polluted by poop can lead to fish dying inland and on the seashore. Wildlife drinking the poop-polluted water can also die from disease.

Too much poop!

We must think about the whole circle of poop: where we can reduce, and how we can reuse and recycle this natural bi-product.

It's about getting the poop balance right.

Poop protection: what can be dung?

Poop is everywhere on Earth! Let's talk about lots of different ways to work with poop.

Poop food for thought

Around the world, people are thinking about how to recycle more poop as a **sustainable fertilizer**. As a fertilizer, poop can continue to help feed living things without piling up.

Creating **less poop overall** is also a helpful way forward! For example, eating less meat cuts down on the amount of animals that are farmed and the poop they make.

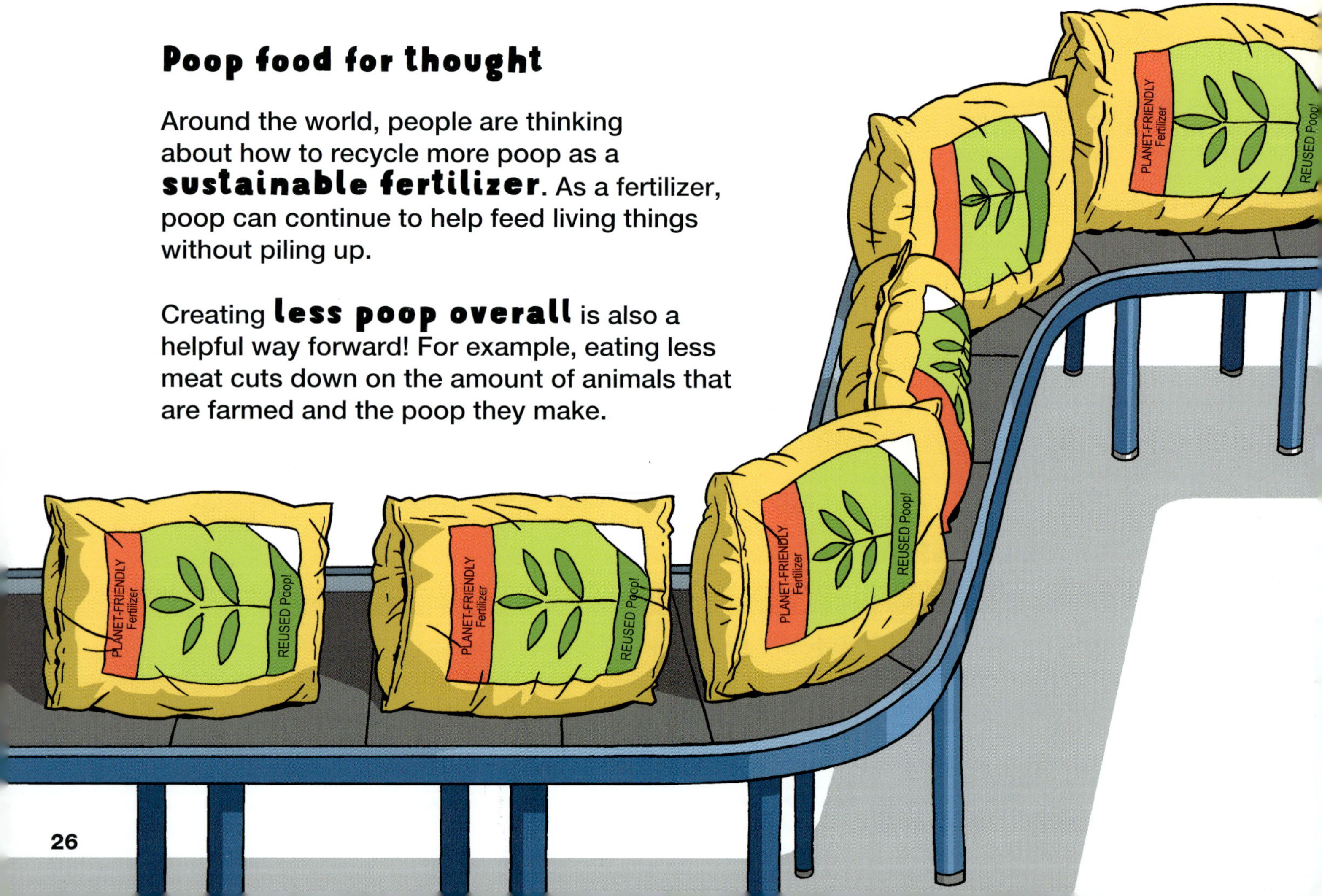

Poop friends

Poop needs help! By working with nature, and using **fewer chemicals**, lots of farmers and industries are helping to maintain all those poop-munching heroes, such as the dung beetle.

Leaving our decomposers to safely deal with the poop means less methane that adds to climate change.

Poop is power!

It's not just your poop in the bathroom. The way we **process** and **treat** poop affects the planet's ecosystems and our future.

What you can do ...

Poop the right thing!

Remember to flush only poop, pee, and paper. By keeping the sewers full of only biodegradable materials, you're helping bacteria to get working to process that poop.

Be a scatologist

How about an owl-pellet hunt? Get to know the animals in your local area through this amazing source of scientific information.

WITH PERMISSION and HELP FROM AN ADULT:

- Look for owl pellets at the base of tall trees, or perhaps on the floor of a barn where you've seen barn owls fly.
- Note the size, shape, and color on a piece of paper.
- Break it apart with a stick and see what's inside. You might see lots of tiny bones from its prey!
- Report your findings to a local conservation group or prepare a poster for your classmates!

... for poop!

Be more like the dung beetle

Poop and renew! Perhaps you can find out about a local poop-composting project, or start your own with the help of an adult? Inform and inspire others to do what's best with this never-ending resource.

Keep talking about poop!

WARNING: Poop is great stuff, but **never** handle it with bare hands or without adult supervision, and **always** be sure to wash your hands if you have been **anywhere** around it!

Glossary

Bacteria – one-celled living things of which there are many, many species. Some species of bacteria can cause disease, while others do not.

Biodiversity – all the variety of life, whether plants, animals, fungi or microorganisms, as well as the ecosystems they form and the habitats in which they live.

Carnivore – an animal that mostly eats other animals.

Climate change – the process of our planet heating up and our world weather changing. This is due to many reasons, including methane escaping into the atmosphere. For example, methane is released as livestock dung breaks down.

Compost – decayed, organic material used as a fertilizer for growing plants.

Decomposers – something that breaks down materials into simpler substances.

Ecosystem – all the organisms living in a certain area, and how they interact with that environment to form a natural community.

Fertilizer – a substance containing nutrients that plants need to grow. Fertilizer can be organic (poop) or synthetic (made artificially by scientists through a chemical process).

Fiber – a type of carbohydrate found in foods, such as whole grains, beans, fruit, and vegetables, which the body can't digest. It helps your food to move through your digestive system.

Greenhouse gas – gas in Earth's atmosphere that traps heat and keeps the Earth warm. Too much of these gases, such as methane or carbon dioxide, means the Earth heats up too much.

Habitat – the home environment for plants and animals or other organisms. Examples of habitats include: desert, meadow, and woodland.

Herbivore – animals that only eat plants.

Microbes – the tiny living microorganisms you cannot see with the naked eye, for example bacteria and viruses.

Microbiome – the group of good microbes inside our guts, which keep our bodies healthy.

Nutrients – any substance that plants, animals, or fungi need in order to live and grow.

Nymph – the young of some insects.

Phytoplankton – a type of algae that provides food for a range of animals in fresh water and the oceans.

Pollutant – any substance that makes soil, water, or air dirty and unhealthy, such as raw sewage or plastic.

Zooplankton – very small animals, such as water mites and crustaceans, that float near the surface of water and provide food for other animals.

Further info

Find out more about the icky bits of nature!

Books:

Extreme Poop Facts by Noah Leatherland (Bearport Publishing Company, 2025)

Scat: The Incredible Science of Wildlife Poop by Anita Sanchez (Holiday House, 2025)

Whose Poop Is That? by Darrin P. Lunde (Charlesbridge, 2025)

Websites:
https://kids.nationalgeographic.com/books/article/create-compost
Learn more about making compost

www.nhm.ac.uk/discover/what-is-a-coprolite.html
to learn more about dinosaur poop

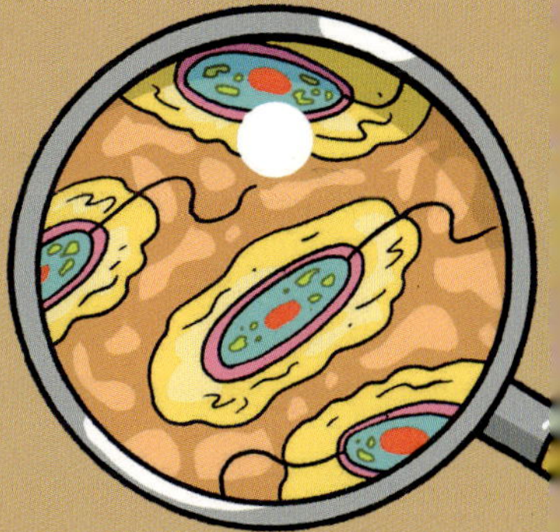

INDEX